초등 영어독해를 쉽고 재미있게!

똑똑한 초등영어독해 jump ❷ [개정판]

초등 영어독해를 쉽고 재미있게!
똑똑한 초등영어독해 jump ❷ [개정판]

2007년 11월 06일 초판 1쇄 발행
2024년 4월 17일 개정 1쇄 인쇄
2024년 4월 25일 개정 1쇄 발행

지은이 국제어학연구소 영어학부
감수 Jenny Kim
그림 조한유
펴낸이 이규인
펴낸곳 국제어학연구소 출판부

출판등록 2010년 1월 18일 제302-2010-000006호
주소 서울특별시 마포구 대흥로4길 49, 1층(용강동 월명빌딩)
Tel (02) 704-0900 **팩시밀리** (02) 703-5117
홈페이지 www.bookcamp.co.kr
e-mail changbook1@hanmail.net
ISBN 979-11-9875871-2 13740
정가 13,000원

영어의 기초를 다져 주는
magic 시리즈

초등 영어 독해를 쉽고 재미있게!

똑똑한 초등 영어독해

Jump ② [개정판]

글 국제어학연구소 영어학부 | 감수 Jenny Kim | 그림 조한유

ILR 국제어학연구소

머리말

언어를 익히는 것에 있어서 책을 많이 있는 것처럼 중요한 것은 없습니다. 문화, 사회, 과학, 예술 등 여러 분야의 책을 읽으면 자신의 지식을 넓힐 수 있고, 언어를 사용함에 있어서도 풍부한 에너지를 키울 수 있습니다. 영어를 배우는 과정에서도 이러한 과정은 필요합니다. 긴 내용의 책을 한 권씩 읽는 것도 좋지만, 짧은 내용의 지문을 읽으면서 영어의 지식을 넓히는 것도 매우 도움이 됩니다.

이 책은 아이들이 여러 분야의 내용들을 짧은 지문을 통해서 읽어보는 것에 중점을 두었습니다. 또한 자신이 읽은 내용이 어떤 내용인지 스스로 생각하여 문제를 풀어보고, 그 지문에 나온 단어들을 익히도록 구성하였습니다. 천천히 한 단원씩 읽어 나가면서 글의 내용을 자신의 지식으로 만들 수 있기를 바랍니다.

영어를 학습함에 있어서는 자기 스스로 하려는 자세가 매우 중요합니다. 자기 수준에 적합한 책을 선정하여 듣고, 읽고, 생각하는 것을 반복하여 자신의 영어 지식으로 만들어야 합니다. 그래서 이 교재는 단계별로 구성하였습니다. 자신의 수준에 알맞은 것을 골라서 스스로 학습하는 자세를 키워나가기를 바랍니다.

이 책의 구성

Before Reading

스토리에 대한 이해도를 높이기 위하여 새로운 단어와 중요 표현을 미리 익혀요.

Story

앞에서 배운 단어와 표현을 생각하면서 스토리를 이해해요.

Vocabulary

배운 단어들을 2가지 형태의 쓰기 문제를 통해 확인해요.

After Reading

스토리를 얼마나 이해했는지 자신의 실력을 체크해 봐요.

Story Comprehension

스토리에 대한 이해도를 종합적으로 확인해 봐요.

차례

Before Reading

New Words

draw

puppy

cute

butterfly

beautiful

flower

colorful

lovely

painter

Key Expression

> **What a beautiful butterfly!**

❶ What a _____ _____! (cute/kitten)

❷ What a _____ _____! (large/tree)

Annie likes to draw.

My younger sister Annie likes to draw.

She draws a puppy.

What a cute puppy!

She draws a butterfly.

What a beautiful butterfly!

She draws flowers.

What colorful flowers they are!

She draws herself.

What a lovely girl!

She is a good painter.

Vocabulary

Write the Words

| puppy | flower | beautiful | lovely | painter | butterfly |

Unscramble the Letters

After Reading

Look and Check

a. Annie draws a kitten.

b. Annie draws a puppy.

a. Annie draws a butterfly.

b. Annie draws a dragonfly.

a. Annie draws herself.

b. Annie draws her brother.

Number the Sentences

a. What a cute puppy! _____

b. What a beautiful butterfly! _____

c. What colorful flowers they are! _____

Choose the Correct Words

1 My _____ sister Annie likes to draw.

    a. older   b. younger

2 _____ a beautiful butterfly!

    a. How   b. What

3 She is a good _____.

    a. painting   b. painter

Check True or False

1 What a lovely girl!

    T ☐   F ☐

2 What a beautiful butterfly!

    T ☐   F ☐

3 What a colorful puppy!

    T ☐   F ☐

Story Comprehension

1 What's the main idea?

   a. Annie's puppy

   b. Annie's dream

   c. Annie's drawings

2 Who is Annie?

   a. The boy's girlfriend

   b. The boy's older sister

   c. The boy's younger sister

3 What does Annie like to do?

   a. reading books

   b. drawing pictures

   c. taking a walk with a puppy

4 What does not Annie draw?

   a. a puppy   b. a butterfly   c. a house

5 Is Annie a good painter?

   a. Yes, she is.   b. No, she isn't.

Before Reading

New Words

weather

warm

spring

cool

autumn

cloudy

windy

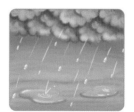

rainy

Key Expression

We have various weather.

① We eat _____ food every day.

② We have _____ plants in our garden.

Weather

We have various weather.

Warm in spring.

Hot in summer.

Cool in autumn.

Cold in winter.

Weather is always changing.

Sometimes it's sunny.

Sometimes it's cloudy.

Sometimes it is windy and rainy.

Sometimes it is snowy.

Vocabulary

Write the Words

| spring windy autumn cloudy rainy warm |

①

②

③

_____

_____

_____

④

⑤

⑥

_____

_____

_____

Unscramble the Letters

①

w a
e t r
h e

_____

②

o o
c l

_____

After Reading

Look and Check

1.
a. Warm in spring.
b. Cool in spring.

2.
a. Hot in summer.
b. Warm in summer.

3.
a. Cold in winter.
b. Cool in winter.

Number the Sentences

  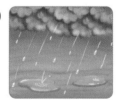

1   2   3

a. Sometimes it's sunny. _____

b. Sometimes it's rainy. _____

c. Sometimes it's cloudy. _____

Choose the Correct Words

❶ We _____ various weather.

    a. has   b. have

❷ The weather is always _____.

    a. change   b. changing

❸ Sometimes it is windy _____ rainy.

    a. and   b. but

Check True or False

❶ We have same weather.

    T ☐   F ☐

❷ Cool in autumn.

    T ☐   F ☐

❸ Hot in summer.

    T ☐   F ☐

Story Comprehension

1 What's the main idea?

   a. Four seasons

   b. Various weather

   c. Changing on Earth

2 How's the weather in summer?

   a. hot   b. cool   c. cold

3 How's the weather in winter?

   a. warm   b. hot   c. cold

4 We have _____ weather.

   a. only one   b. two kinds of   c. various

5 What's not true?

   a. Weather is always changing.

   b. Sometimes it is windy and rainy.

   c. Sometimes it is snowy in summer.

Before Reading

New Words

weird

late

school

listen

class

curious

daydream

imaginative

Key Expression

He is always late for school.

① You _____ always _____ for class.

② Her boss _____ always _____ for meeting.

Eric is a weird boy.

Eric is a weird boy.

He is different from other boys.

He is always late for school.

He often doesn't listen in class.

And he often daydreams.

His teacher says,

"Eric is the worst boy in our school."

But he isn't the worst boy.

He is just very curious about everything.

And he is just an imaginative boy.

He is never a weird boy.

Vocabulary

Write the Words

| weird   listen   curious   imaginative   school   late |

①
_____

②
_____

③
_____

④
_____

⑤
_____

⑥
_____

Unscramble the Letters

①
a c
s l
s

②
d y
a r e m
a d

After Reading

Look and Check

a. Eric is a smart boy.

b. Eric is a weird boy.

a. Eric listens carefully in class.

b. Eric doesn't listen in class.

a. Eric is a shy boy.

b. Eric is an imaginative boy.

Number the Sentences

a. He is always late for school. _____

b. He is often in a daydream. _____

c. His teacher says, "He is the worst boy." _____

Choose the Correct Words

1 Eric doesn't _____ in class.

    a. listen   b. listens

2 Eric is just _____ imaginative boy.

    a. a   b. an

3 Eric is always _____ for school.

    a. late   b. lately

Check True or False

1 Eric is different from other boys.

    T ☐   F ☐

2 Eric is never late for school.

    T ☐   F ☐

3 His teacher says, "Eric is the best boy in our school."

    T ☐   F ☐

Story Comprehension

1 What's the main idea?

    a. A smart boy

    b. The worst boy

    c. An imaginative boy

2 How often is Eric late for school?

    a. sometimes   b. often   c. always

3 Why is Eric late for school?

    a. Because he is very lazy.

    b. Because he is always sleepy.

    c. Because he is very curious about everything.

4 Why doesn't Eric listen in class?

    a. Because he often daydreams.

    b. Because he falls asleep in class.

    c. Because he doesn't want to study.

5 In conclusion, what is he like?

    a. He is a weird boy.

    b. He is just an imaginative boy.

    c. He is the worst boy in his class.

Before Reading

New Words

wolf

travel

through

forest

otter

follow

stream

drink

Key Expression

They arrived at the stream.

❶ We will soon _____ _____ the station.

❷ He _____ _____ the farm yesterday.

A wolf and an otter

A wolf traveled through a great forest.

He was very thirsty and hungry.

He met an otter.

"Where is water?" said the wolf.

"Follow me." said the otter.

The wolf followed the otter.

They arrived at the stream.

The wolf drank some water.

The otter also gave some food to the wolf.

The wolf made friends with the otter.

Vocabulary

Write the Words

| travel | forest | otter | follow | wolf | stream |

①

②

③

④

⑤

⑥

Unscramble the Letters

①

h t
o g h
r u

②

k r
i d n

After Reading

Look and Check

a. The wolf ate the food.

b. The wolf drank the water.

a. The wolf was very thirsty.

b. The wolf was very sleepy.

a. The otter gave the wolf some food.

b. The otter gave the wolf some trees.

Number the Sentences

a. The wolf met an otter. _____

b. The wolf traveled through a forest. _____

c. The wolf was very hungry. _____

Choose the Correct Words

1. "_____ is water?" said the wolf.

   a. What   b. Where

2. The wolf and the otter arrived _____ the stream.

   a. at   b. into

3. The otter gave food _____ the wolf.

   a. of   b. to

Check True or False

1. The wolf drank some water.

   T ☐   F ☐

2. The wolf traveled through a city.

   T ☐   F ☐

3. The otter also gave some food to the wolf.

   T ☐   F ☐

Story Comprehension

1. What's the main idea?

   a. The wolf's new friend

   b. Traveling a great forest

   c. A thirsty and hungry wolf

2. Where did the wolf travel?

   a. city   b. forest   c. mountain

3. Who helped the wolf?

   a. a fox   b. a lion   c. an otter

4. Where did they arrive at?

   a. sea   b. river   c. stream

5. What is not true?

   a. The wolf was very hungry.

   b. The wolf followed the otter.

   c. The wolf swam in the stream.

Before Reading

New Words

little

big

taller

much taller

skateboard

bike

tricycle

grow

Key Expression

Jane is taller than Judy.

① Paul is _____ than Peter. (old)

② Cindy is _____ than Sally. (short)

Judy wants to grow up.

Judy is a little girl.

She has a big sister and a big brother.

Her sister, Jane is taller than Judy.

And her brother, Jake is much taller.

Jake has a nice skateboard.

Jane has a big bike.

Judy has a little tricycle.

Judy wants to grow up.

She wants to ride a big bike.

She wants to ride a skateboard.

Vocabulary

Write the Words

| grow | big | skateboard | bike | much taller | taller |

①

②

③

④

⑤

⑥

Unscramble the Letters

①

t t l l i e

②

t c e l r i y c

After Reading

Look and Check

a. Judy has a big bike.

b. Judy has a little tricycle.

a. Jake has a big bike.

b. Jake has a nice skateboard.

a. Her sister, Jane is taller than Judy.

b. Her sister, Jane is shorter than Judy.

Number the Sentences

a. She has a big brother. _____

b. She wants to ride a big bike. _____

c. She has a big sister and a big brother. _____

Choose the Correct Words

① Judy is a _____ girl.

     a. big   b. little

② Her sister, Jane is _____ than Judy.

     a. tall   b. taller

③ Judy wants to _____ a big bike.

     a. ride   b. rides

Check True or False

① Judy has a big sister and a big brother.

     T ☐   F ☐

② Judy is Jane's big sister.

     T ☐   F ☐

③ Jake is Judy's big brother.

     T ☐   F ☐

Story Comprehension

① What's the main idea?

    a. Jane's wish   b. Judy's wish   c. Jake's wish

② Who is the tallest of the three?

    a. Judy   b. Jane   c. Jake

③ Who is the youngest of the three?

    a. Judy   b. Jane   c. Jake

④ What does Judy have?

    a. a big bike

    b. a little tricycle

    c. a nice skateboard

⑤ What does Judy want?

    a. She wants to ride a car.

    b. She wants to grow fast.

    c. She wants to have a nice tricycle.

Before Reading

New Words

country

yard

playground

pond

swings

seesaw

trampoline

fish

Key Expression

There are fish in the pond.

❶ There are _____ in the fence. (deer)

❷ There are _____ in the farm. (sheep)

Grandpa's yard

My grandparents live in the country.

There is a big yard in their house.

There is a playground in the yard.

There is a small pond, too.

My grandpa made them for us.

There is a trampoline, a seesaw,

and swings in the playground.

There are some fish in the pond.

We love to play in the playground.

And we love to watch fish in the pond.

We are very happy to be there.

Vocabulary

Write the Words

| pond | trampoline | swings | yard | playground | seesaw |

1

2

3

_____

4

5

6

_____

Unscramble the Letters

1
t o
c u n
r y

2
i s
h f

After Reading

Look and Check

   a. My grandparents live in the city.

   b. My grandparents live in the country.

   a. There is a big yard in their house.

   b. There is a small yard in their house.

   a. There are some fish in the pond.

   b. There are some plants in the pond.

Number the Sentences

a. There is a trampoline in the playground. _____

b. There is a small pond. _____

c. There are swings in the playground. _____

Choose the Correct Words

1 There _____ a big yard in their house.

    a. is   b. are

2 And there is a small pond, _____.

    a. too   b. both

3 We are _____ happy to be there.

    a. much   b. very

Check True or False

1 My parents live in the country.

    T ☐   F ☐

2 There is a small pond in the yard.

    T ☐   F ☐

3 We love to play in the garden.

    T ☐   F ☐

Story Comprehension

1 What's the main idea?

   a. My grandparents' pond

   b. My grandparents' yard

   c. My grandparents' house

2 Where do the boy's grandparents live?

   a. city   b. island   c. country

3 Where is the playground?

   a. in the yard   b. in the room   c. in the pond

4 What is not in the playground?

   a. slide   b. swings   c. seesaw

5 Who made the playground and the pond?

   a. the boy's dad

   b. the boy's uncle

   c. the boy's grandpa

Before Reading

New Words

famous

movie star

universe

astronaut

rich

businessman

piano

pianist

Key Expression

Sometimes he wants to be famous.

❶ I _____ _____ _____ happy.

❷ Sally _____ _____ _____ a dancer.

Kevin has many dreams.

Kevin often changes his dream.

Sometimes he wants to be famous.

So he wants to be a movie star.

Sometimes he wants to know about the universe.

So he wants to be an astronaut.

Sometimes he wants to be rich.

So he wants to be a businessman.

And sometimes he wants to play the piano.

So he wants to be a pianist.

Vocabulary

Write the Words

universe movie star astronaut businessman pianist rich

①

②

③

④

⑤

⑥

Unscramble the Letters

①

a o
p i n

②

m o u
f a s

After Reading

Look and Check

a. He wants to be a dancer.

b. He wants to be a movie star.

a. He wants to be a pilot.

b. He wants to be an astronaut.

a. He wants to be a doctor.

b. He wants to be a businessman.

Number the Sentences

a. He wants to play the piano. _____

b. He wants to be rich. _____

c. He wants to be famous. _____

Choose the Correct Words

1. Kevin often _____ his dream.

   a. change   b. changes

2. He wants to _____ about the universe.

   a. be   b. know

3. He wants to be _____ astronaut.

   a. a   b. an

Check True or False

1. Kevin never changes his dream.

   T ☐   F ☐

2. Sometimes he wants to be rich.

   T ☐   F ☐

3. Sometimes he wants to fly in the sky.

   T ☐   F ☐

Story Comprehension

1. What's the main idea?

   a. Kevin's job   b. Kevin's life   c. Kevin's dream

2. How often does Kevin's dream change?

   a. never   b. often   c. always

3. Which is not Kevin's dream?

   a. To be a teacher

   b. To be a movie star

   c. To be a businessman

4. What is not true?

   a. Kevin often changes his dream.

   b. Sometimes he wants to be rich.

   c. Sometimes he wants to know about animals.

5. Kevin has many _____.

   a. books   b. dreams   c. friends

Before Reading

New Words

join

camp

hike

top

mountain

dinner

tent

snore

awake

Key Expression

I joined a summer camp.

1 I'd like to _____ the club.

2 Do you want to _____ us?

He began to snore.

Jack and I joined a summer camp.

We hiked to the top of the mountain.

And then we cooked dinner by ourselves.

So we were very tired.

Jack and I went to our tent.

Jack soon fell asleep, but I couldn't.

Because he began to snore.

I couldn't stand this.

So I got up and went out of the tent.

I was wide awake all night.

Vocabulary

Write the Words

| camp | top | tent | snore | hike | awake |

① _____

② _____

③ _____

④ _____

⑤ _____

⑥ _____

Unscramble the Letters

① n d
r i n e
_____

② o j
n i
_____

After Reading

Look and Check

a. Jack and I had a long trip.

b. Jack and I joined a summer camp.

a. Jack and I went to our tent.

b. Jack and I went to my room.

a. Jack began to smile.

b. Jack began to snore.

Number the Sentences

a. We cooked dinner by ourselves. _____

b. I went out of the tent. _____

c. We were very tired. _____

Choose the Correct Words

❶ Jack soon fell _____, but I couldn't.

    a. sleep   b. asleep

❷ Because he _____ to snore.

    a. began   b. finished

❸ I _____ stand this.

    a. didn't   b. couldn't

Check True or False

❶ Jack and I joined a tennis club.

    T ☐   F ☐

❷ We hiked to the top of the mountain.

    T ☐   F ☐

❸ I was wide awake all night.

    T ☐   F ☐

Story Comprehension

1. What's the main idea?

   a. Hiking

   b. Cooking dinner

   c. Friend's snoring

2. What did they do that day?

   a. hiking and cooking

   b. hiking and swimming

   c. cooking and swimming

3. How did they feel after cooking dinner?

   a. full   b. happy   c. tired

4. Who did snore?

   a. dog   b. Jack   c. both

5. Why couldn't the boy sleep?

   a. Because Jack snored.

   b. Because the boy was sick.

   c. Because the boy was so tired.

Before Reading

New Words

timid

brave

nearby

step

stone

breath

scared

Key Expression

You can do it.

1 I _____ swim well.

2 She _____ play the piano.

Sam wasn't scared.

Sam was a timid boy.

And his friend, Jake was a brave boy.

One day, they went to the stream nearby.

There were stepping stones in the stream.

Jake was jumping on the stones.

Jake said, "Come on, Sam. You can do it."

Sam took a deep breath.

"I can do it," said Sam.

And he jumped on the stones, too.

At last, he did it.

Sam felt happy.

Sam wasn't scared.

Vocabulary

Write the Words

stone	brave	nearby	timid	step

①

②

③

_____

_____

_____

④

⑤

_____

_____

Unscramble the Letters

①

b h
e r a
t

②

s d
c a e
r

After Reading

Look and Check

a. Sam was a timid boy.

b. Sam was a brave boy.

a. Sam was jumping on the stones.

b. Sam threw the stones to the stream.

a. They went to the stream nearby .

b. They went to the mountain nearby.

Number the Sentences

a. Jake said, "Come on, Sam." _____

b. "I can do it," said Sam. _____

c. He felt good. _____

Choose the Correct Words

① Sam was a _____ boy.

    a. timid   b. cheerful

② They went to the stream _____.

    a. far   b. nearby

③ There _____ stepping stones in the stream.

    a. was   b. were

Check True or False

❶ Sam visited Jake's home.

    T ☐   F ☐

❷ Jake was a brave boy.

    T ☐   F ☐

❸ Sam was jumping on the fence.

    T ☐   F ☐

Story Comprehension

1 What's the main idea?

  a. A timid boy, Jake

  b. A brave boy, Sam

  c. Sam isn't a timid boy anymore.

2 What character did Sam have?

  a. timid   b. brave   c. active

3 What were there in the stream?

  a. many fish   b. dirty water   c. stepping stones

4 Who jumped on the stones first?

  a. Sam   b. Jake

5 What is true?

  a. Jake jumped on the stones.

  b. Sam didn't jump on the stones.

  c. Sam and Jake went to the forest nearby.

Before Reading

New Words

birthday

purple

giraffe

glad

gift

kiss

cookie

Key Expression

Her dad gave Judy a purple giraffe.

1 She _____ me a _____. (gave/gift)

2 They _____ her a _____. (gave/computer)

I love you, Purple Giraffe.

Today was Cindy's birthday.

Her dad gave Cindy a purple giraffe.

She was very glad about this gift.

Cindy loved the purple giraffe.

Cindy said, "I love you, Purple Giraffe."

She kissed Purple Giraffe.

She ate cookies with him.

She read books with him.

She played with him all the time.

And Cindy went to bed with him.

Vocabulary

Write the Words

| gift | cookie | birthday | purple | giraffe |

①

②

③

_____

④

⑤

_____

Unscramble the Letters

①
d
g   a
l

②
i
s   s
k

After Reading

Look and Check

a. Dad gave Cindy a teddy bear.
b. Dad gave Cindy a purple giraffe.

a. Today was Christmas.
b. Today was Cindy's birthday.

a. Cindy went to bed with his dad.
b. Cindy went to bed with Purple Giraffe.

Number the Sentences

a. She kissed Purple Giraffe. _____

b. She ate cookies with Purple Giraffe. _____

c. She was very glad about this gift. _____

Choose the Correct Words

1 Today was _____ birthday.

      a. Cindy   b. Cindy's

2 She ate cookies _____ him.

      a. with   b. without

3 She _____ with him all the time.

      a. play   b. played

Check True or False

1 Her mom gave Cindy a purple giraffe.

      T ☐   F ☐

2 Cindy didn't like Purple Giraffe.

      T ☐   F ☐

3 Cindy went to bed with Purple Giraffe.

      T ☐   F ☐

Story Comprehension

1 What's the main idea?

   a. Cindy's toys

   b. Cindy's birthday

   c. Cindy's Purple Giraffe

2 Whose birthday was today?

   a. Cindy   b. Dad   c. Purple Giraffe

3 Who gave Cindy a purple giraffe?

   a. Mom   b. Dad   c. Uncle

4 How did Cindy feel about Dad's gift?

   a. She was very glad.

   b. She was very sad.

   c. She was very angry.

5 What is not true?

   a. Cindy loved Purple Giraffe.

   b. Cindy went to bed with Purple Giraffe.

   c. Cindy went to school with Purple Giraffe.

Before Reading

New Words

television

show

singer

dancer

drama

act

actor

entertainer

Key Expression

She loves to watch TV.

1 Eric _____ _____ _____ the guitar. (play)

2 I _____ _____ _____ Korean History. (study)

Annie loves to watch television.

Annie loves to watch television.

Especially, she likes the music show.

Annie sings a song like a pop singer on TV.

And she dances like a back dancer.

She dances and sings quite well.

Annie often watches dramas on TV.

Annie acts like an actor.

She acts quite well, too.

Annie's friends like her dancing and singing.

She will be a good entertainer.

Vocabulary

Write the Words

| actor | entertainer | act | dancer | television | show |

_____

_____

_____

_____

_____

_____

Unscramble the Letters

g i
n s e
r

r a
d
m a

After Reading

Look and Check

a. Annie loves to watch television.

b. Annie loves to watch sports game.

a. Annie acts quite well.

b. Annie dances like a back dancer.

a. Annie's friends like her dancing.

b. Annie's friends hate her dancing.

Number the Sentences

a. Annie sings quite well. _____

b. Annie dances quite well. _____

c. Annie acts like an actor. _____

Choose the Correct Words

1 Annie loves to _____ television.

    a. watch   b. watches

2 Annie's _____ like her dancing and singing.

    a. friend   b. friends

3 She will _____ a good entertainer.

    a. is   b. be

Check True or False

1 Especially, Annie likes the music show.

    T ☐   F ☐

2 She dances like a ballet dancer.

    T ☐   F ☐

3 Annie seldom watches dramas on TV.

    T ☐   F ☐

Story Comprehension

1. What's the main idea?

   a. Watching TV

   b. Annie's talent

   c. Singers and dancers

2. What does Annie love to watch?

   a. ballet   b. television   c. sport games

3. Annie sings a song like _____.

   a. a rapper   b. a chorus   c. a pop singer

4. She will be a good _____.

   a. announcer   b. entertainer   c. sport player

5. What is not true?

   a. Annie likes to sing.

   b. Annie likes to act like an actor.

   c. Annie's parents like her dancing and singing.

Before Reading

New Words

dark

go back

shortcut

down

track

dangerous

train

pass

Key Expression

It was getting dark.

1 My dad is _____ _____. (old)

2 It was _____ _____. (cold)

They were fine.

A boy and a girl went on a picnic.

They had a wonderful time.

But it was getting dark.

They had to go back home.

They decided to take the shortcut.

They walked down the tracks.

It was very dangerous.

Because trains come sometimes.

A few minutes later, a train came.

They got off the tracks.

The train passed, they were fine.

Vocabulary

Write the Words

go back	shortcut	down	dark	dangerous	train

①

②

③

④

⑤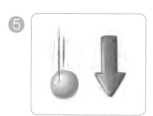

⑥

Unscramble the Letters

① 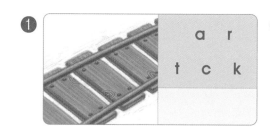 a r t c k

②  p s s a

After Reading

Look and Check

a. A boy and a girl went on a picnic.

b. A boy and a girl went to see a movie.

a. It was getting hot.

b. It was getting dark.

a. They got off the tracks.

b. They walked down the tracks.

Number the Sentences

a. A train passed. _____

b. A train appeared. _____

c. They walked down the tracks. _____

Choose the Correct Words

① It was _____ dark.

      a. get   b. getting

② They had to _____ back home.

      a. go   b. going

③ They decided to _____ the shortcut.

      a. take   b. took

Check True or False

❶ A boy and a girl went on a picnic.

      T ☐   F ☐

❷ They had to go back to school.

      T ☐   F ☐

❸ A few minutes later, a bus came.

      T ☐   F ☐

Story Comprehension

❶ What's the main idea?

   a. A train

   b. A picnic

   c. The dangerous tracks

❷ How many boys and girls went on a picnic?

   a. two   b. three   c. four

❸ Why did they decide to take the shortcut?

   a. It was too early.

   b. It was getting dark.

   c. There weren't other ways.

❹ What came on the track?

   a. a bus   b. a train   c. a plane

❺ What is not true?

   a. They were hurt.

   b. They decided to take the shortcut.

   c. A boy and a girl had a wonderful time.

Before Reading

New Words

monkey

leopard

forget

nap

look for

lunch

catch

run away

Key Expression

He tried to catch all.

❶ She _____ _____ jump up.

❷ They _____ _____ forget about it.

One monkey is not enough.

Two monkeys played on the tree.

They had to be careful about leopards.

But the monkeys forgot about leopards,

because they were too sleepy.

They both took a nap.

A hungry leopard was looking for lunch.

At last, he found two monkeys.

He was very hungry.

He thought, "One monkey is not enough."

He wanted two monkeys.

He tried to catch both.

But two monkeys ran away.

Vocabulary

Write the Words

| nap | leopard | lunch | look for | catch | run away |

①

②

③

_____

④

⑤

⑥

_____

Unscramble the Letters

①

②

After Reading

Look and Check

①
    a. Two monkeys played in the river.
    b. Two monkeys played on the tree.

②
    a. A leopard was very happy.
    b. A leopard was very hungry.

③
    a. A leopard tired to catch a monkey.
    b. A leopard tried to catch two monkeys.

Number the Sentences

①    ②    ③

a. A leopard was looking for lunch. _____

b. Monkeys both took a nap. _____

c. Two monkeys ran away. _____

Choose the Correct Words

❶ The monkeys had to be careful _____ leopards.

     a. above   b. about

❷ One monkey is _____ enough.

     a. no   b. not

❸ A leopard tried to catch _____.

     a. both   b. the only one

Check True or False

❶ Two monkeys played on the tree.

     T ☐   F ☐

❷ They had to be careful about rabbits.

     T ☐   F ☐

❸ A leopard thought, "One monkey is not enough."

     T ☐   F ☐

Story Comprehension

① What's the main idea?

   a. Stupid monkeys

   b. A stupid leopard

   c. A leopard and the tree

② Where were the monkeys?

   a. in the zoo   b. on the tree   c. in the house

③ What was the leopard looking for?

   a. He was looking for lunch.

   b. He was looking for water.

   c. He was looking for friends.

④ What did the leopard find?

   a. trees   b. rabbits   c. monkeys

⑤ What is not true?

   a. The leopard was very hungry.

   b. The leopard thought, "One monkey is not enough."

   c. The leopard catched two monkeys.

Before Reading

New Words

winter

morning

window

snow

cover

breakfast

put on

snowsuit

snowman

Key Expression

They **put on** their snowsuit.

❶ We _____ _____ our shoes.

❷ I _____ _____ my hat.

One winter morning

One winter morning, Sally woke up.

She looked out the window.

It was snowing.

Snow covered everything.

She ate breakfast quickly.

After breakfast, she put on her snowsuit.

And she ran out of the house.

She met her friend.

She made a snowman with her friend.

And they had a snowball fight.

It was very cold, but it was very fun.

Vocabulary

Write the Words

| window | cover | breakfast | snowman | winter | put on |

1

2

3

4

5

6

Unscramble the Letters

1

    n m
    o r i
    n g

2

    w
    n o
    s

After Reading

Look and Check

❶
a. One winter morning Sally woke up.
b. One winter morning Sally went to bed.

❷
a. Snow covered nothing.
b. Snow covered everything.

❸
a. They made a snowman.
b. They had a snowball fight.

Number the Sentences

  ❷  ❸

a. She looked out the window. _____

b. She made a snowman. _____

c. She put on her snowsuit. _____

Choose the Correct Words

1. One winter morning, Sally _____ up.

    a. wake   b. woke

2. _____ breakfast, she put on her snowsuit.

    a. After   b. Before

3. They _____ a snowball fight.

    a. has   b. had

Check True or False

1. Sally opened the window.

    T ☐   F ☐

2. It was snowing.

    T ☐   F ☐

3. After breakfast, she put on her sandals.

    T ☐   F ☐

Story Comprehension

❶ What's the main idea?

   a. Snow   b. Snowman   c. Snowball fight

❷ What was the weather like?

   a. sunny   b. cloudy   c. snowy

❸ What did Sally do after breakfast?

   a. She stayed at home.

   b. She washed the dishes.

   c. She put on her snowsuit.

❹ What did Sally do outside?

   a. Sally ate breakfast.

   b. Sally ran with the dog.

   c. Sally made a snowman.

❺ It was very cold, _____ it was very fun.

   a. and   b. but   c. then

Before Reading

New Words

evening

busy

spaghetti

bring

beef

tomato

onion

plate

Key Expression

They **were making** the spaghetti.

❶ I _____ _____ English. (study)

❷ She _____ _____ her room. (clean)

Rick was helping Mom.

It was evening.
Rick and Mom were busy.
They were making spaghetti.
Mom said, "Son, can you bring some beef?"
"Sure, Mom." Rick said.
And Rick brought some beef.
Mom said, "Can you bring some tomatoes?"
Mom said, "Can you bring some onions?"
Spaghetti was done.
Mom said, "Can you bring some plates?"
They ate spaghetti for dinner.
It was very delicious.

Vocabulary

Write the Words

plate	tomato	onion	busy	spaghetti	beef

①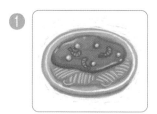

②

③

_____

_____

_____

④

⑤

⑥

_____

_____

_____

Unscramble the Letters

①

g n
i r b

②

v n
e e
g n i

After Reading

Look and Check

a. It was morning.

b. It was evening.

②

a. Rick and Mom were free.

b. Rick and Mom were busy.

③

a. They ate the pancake.

b. They ate the spaghetti.

Number the Sentences

❶  ❷  ❸

a. Can you bring some beef? _____

b. Can you bring some tomatoes? _____

c. Can you bring some plates? _____

Choose the Correct Words

❶ They _____ making spaghetti.

      a. was   b. were

❷ _____ you bring some onions?

      a. Does   b. Can

❸ Can you bring some _____?

      a. tomato   b. tomatoes

Check True or False

❶ Rick and Dad were busy.

      T ☐   F ☐

❷ Rick brought some onions.

      T ☐   F ☐

❸ They ate spaghetti for dinner.

      T ☐   F ☐

Story Comprehension

1. What's the main idea?

   a. Eating lunch

   b. Making spaghetti

   c. Bringing some vegetables

2. What were Rick and Mom making?

   a. salad   b. meat balls   c. spaghetti

3. Choose the thing that Rick didn't bring.

   a. bread   b. plates   c. beef

4. They ate the spaghetti for _____.

   a. breakfast   b. lunch   c. dinner

5. What is not true?

   a. It was evening.

   b. Rick helped his mom.

   c. They didn't eat spaghetti.

Before Reading

New Words

mouth

plant

leaf

stem

root

absorb

under

ground

Key Expression

Roots grow under the ground.

① Leaves and stems _____ on the ground.

② Stems _____ upward from their roots.

Plants

Animals drink water and eat food with the mouth.

How do plants drink water and eat food?

Plants have roots, stems and leaves.

Roots grow under the ground.

Leaves and stems grow over the ground.

Roots absorb water and food.

Stems grow upward from their roots.

Roots and stems connect with leaves.

Leaves use the sun's energy to make food.

They work together to make food.

Vocabulary

Write the Words

plant	leaf	stem	root	absorb	ground

①

②

③

④
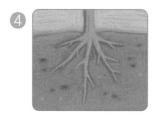

⑤

⑥

Unscramble the Letters

①

d r
u n e

②

m h
o
u t

After Reading

Look and Check

a. Animals drink water with hands.

b. Animals drink water with the mouth.

 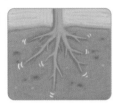

a. Roots grow over the ground.

b. Roots grow under the ground.

a. Plants have leaves and roots.

b. Plants have leaves, stems and roots.

Number the Sentences

a. Leaves use the sun's energy to make food. _____

b. Roots absorb water and food. _____

c. Leaves and stems grow over the ground. _____

Choose the Correct Words

1. Animals drink water and eat food _____ the mouth.

   a. with   b. without

2. Roots absorb water _____ food.

   a. and   b. but

3. Leaves and stems grow _____ the ground.

   a. on   b. over

Check True or False

1. Roots grow on the ground.

   T ☐   F ☐

2. Plants have roots, leaves and stems.

   T ☐   F ☐

3. Stems grow upward from their roots.

   T ☐   F ☐

Story Comprehension

1. What's the main idea?

   a. Stems   b. Plants   c. Animals

2. What do animals drink water with?

   a. hand   b. mouth   c. arm

3. Plants have leaves, _____ and _____.

   a. arms, legs

   b. stems, roots

   c. flowers, bees

4. Leaves use the _____'s energy to make food.

   a. sun   b. moon   c. light

5. What is true?

   a. Roots grow on the ground.

   b. Roots absorb water and food.

   c. Roots are not important.

Before Reading

New Words

zoo

elephant

trunk

deer

photo

antler

dolphin

trainer

Key Expression

Judy wanted to be an animal trainer.

① Jack wants to _____ _____ _____. (astronaut)

② I want to _____ _____ _____. (teacher)

Julie's family went to the zoo.

Julie and her family went to the zoo.

They watched the elephants.

Their trunks were very strong and useful.

They did everything with their trunks.

Julie's mom liked watching the deer.

The antlers of deer were graceful.

Julie's mom took photos of the deer.

Julie and her brother liked watching the dolphins.

The dolphin show was fantastic.

The trainers and dolphins were wonderful.

Julie wanted to be an animal trainer.

Vocabulary

Write the Words

antler   deer   elephant   trainer   dolphin   zoo

①

②

③

_____

④

⑤

⑥

_____

Unscramble the Letters

① t h o p o

_____

② r t n u k

_____

After Reading

Look and Check

1

a. Julie's family went to the zoo.

b. Julie's family went to the beach.

2

a. Its arm was very useful.

b. Its trunk was very useful.

3

a. She took photos of the fish.

b. She took photos of the deer.

Number the Sentences

1  **2**  **3**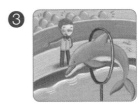

a. The dolphin show was fantastic. _____

b. They watched the elephants. _____

c. The antlers of deer were graceful. _____

Choose the Correct Words

1. Elephants' _____ were very strong and useful.
      a. trunk   b. trunks

2. Julie's mother _____ photos of the deer.
      a. take   b. took

3. Julie wanted _____ an animal trainer.
      a. to do   b. to be

Check True or False

1. Julie's mom liked watching the deer.
      T ☐   F ☐

2. Julie took photos of the deer.
      T ☐   F ☐

3. The dolphin show was fantastic.
      T ☐   F ☐

Story Comprehension

1. What's the main idea?

   a. Watching animals

   b. Taking photos of the deer

   c. Watching the dolphin show

2. Where did Julie's family go?

   a. zoo   b. jungle   c. animal farm

3. Who took photos of the deer?

   a. Julie   b. Julie's brother   c. Julie's mom

4. Which animals have the antlers?

   a. elephant   b. deer   c. dolphin

5. What did Julie want to be?

   a. a vet

   b. a photographer

   c. an animal trainer

Before Reading

New Words

statue

statue of liberty

where

who

when

what

island

French

sculptor

Key Expression

Do you know where the Statue is?

① Do you know _____ the game _____? (when/begin)

② Do you know _____ he _____? (what/have)

Do you know the Statue of Liberty?

Do you know the Statue of Liberty?

Do you know where the Statue is?

Do you know who made the Statue?

Do you know when the Statue was made?

Do you know what the Statue represents?

The Statue is on Liberty Island in New York.

A French sculptor made it.

It was made in 1884.

And it was given to the United States in the same year.

Today, the Statue of Liberty shows freedom.

Vocabulary

Write the Words

| where | when | sculptor | who | what | statue |

1

2

3

4

5

6

Unscramble the Letters

1

n c
e r F
h

2

n
i s
d l a

After Reading

Look and Check

    a. The Statue of Liberty is in London.

    b. The Statue of Liberty is in New York.

    a. A French sculptor made it.

    b. A Japanese sculptor made it.

    a. It was given in the same year.

    b. It was given in the next year.

Number the Sentences

    a. Do you know where the Statue is? _____

    b. Do you know when the Statue was made? _____

    c. Do you know who made the Statue? _____

Choose the Correct Words

① The Statue is _____ Liberty Island.

    a. in   b. on

② Do you know _____ made the Statue?

    a. who   b. where

③ Do you know _____ the Statue represents?

    a. when   b. what

Check True or False

❶ The Statue of Liberty is in the United States.

    T ☐   F ☐

❷ It was given to the United States in 2000.

    T ☐   F ☐

❸ The Statue of Liberty means freedom.

    T ☐   F ☐

Story Comprehension

1 What's the main idea?

   a. The French

   b. Liberty Island

   c. The Statue of Liberty

2 Where is the Statue of Liberty?

   a. France   b. England   c. the United States

3 Who made the Statue of Liberty?

   a. a French sculptor

   b. a American sculptor

   c. a Japanese sculptor

4 When was it given to the United State?

   a. in 1884   b. in 1984   c. in 2000

5 What does the Statue of Liberty represent?

   a. freedom   b. equality   c. happiness

Before Reading

New Words

field

soccer

volleyball

baseball

choose

player

team

win

Key Expression

He can play baseball better than others.

① She is _____ _____ her friends. (prettier)

② Jake plays tennis _____ _____ his classmates. (better)

Story

We had a field day.

Today was a field day.

Peter can't play soccer well.

He can't play volleyball well, either.

But he can play baseball better than others.

So he was chosen as one of the players.

Peter and his team members did their best.

And his team won the baseball game.

Peter was very happy.

His class couldn't win other games.

But Peter was happy to win

the baseball game.

Vocabulary

Write the Words

| volleyball   choose   player   baseball   win   soccer |

①
_____

②
_____

③
_____

④
_____

⑤
_____

⑥
_____

Unscramble the Letters

①
e i
f l d
_____

②
t
m e
a
_____

After Reading

Look and Check

a. Today was Sunday.

b. Today was a field day.

a. Peter can play baseball better than others.

b. Peter can play basketball better than others.

a. His team won the game.

b. His team lost the game.

Number the Sentences

a. Peter can't play soccer well. _____

b. Peter can't play volleyball. _____

c. Peter was very happy. _____

Choose the Correct Words

1. Peter played baseball better _____ others.

    a. then   b. than

2. Peter and his team members did their _____.

    a. best   b. better

3. His class couldn't _____ other games.

    a. won   b. win

Check True or False

1. Peter was happy to win the baseball game.

    T ☐   F ☐

2. Peter's class won the soccer game.

    T ☐   F ☐

3. Peter can play volleyball better than others.

    T ☐   F ☐

Story Comprehension

1 What's the main idea?

   a. A field day

   b. A basketball game

   c. Soccer and baseball

2 What can Peter play well?

   a. soccer   b. volleyball   c. baseball

3 What can't Peter play well?

   a. soccer and baseball

   b. soccer and volleyball

   c. volleyball and baseball

4 Why was Peter happy?

   a. Because his class won all the games.

   b. Because his team won the baseball game.

   c. Because his team members did their best.

5 Did his class win other games?

   a. Yes, they did.

   b. No, they didn't.

Before Reading

New Words

alligator

crocodile

bumpy

leg

strong

reptile

snout

rounded

pointed

Key Expression

> **Their snouts** look **very** different.

❶ My dad _____ very _____. (tired)

❷ The girl _____ very _____. (beautiful)

Alligators and crocodiles

Do you know alligators and crocodiles?

They are reptiles.

They both have bumpy skin.

They have short legs and long, strong tails.

They are both good swimmers.

But their snouts look rather different.

Alligators have rounded snouts.

Crocodiles' snouts are more pointed.

Alligators live only in the United States and China.

Crocodiles live in America, Asia, Africa, and Australia.

Vocabulary

Write the Words

| bumpy | pointed | snout | rounded | strong | reptile |

①

②

③

_____

_____

_____

④

⑤

⑥

_____

_____

_____

Unscramble the Letters

❶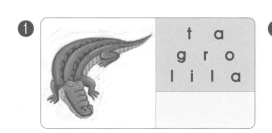

t a
g r o
l i l a

❷

r o c
e c l
i d o

After Reading

Look and Check

a. They have bumpy skin.

b. They have smooth skin.

a. They have short legs.

b. They have long legs.

a. They are both good runners.

b. They are both good swimmers.

Number the Sentences

a. They are reptiles. _____

b. Alligators have rounded snouts. _____

c. Crocodiles' snouts are more pointed. _____

Choose the Correct Words

1. Do you _____ alligators and crocodiles?

   a. know   b. knew

2. Alligators and crocodiles are _____ good swimmers.

   a. two   b. both

3. Crocodiles' snouts are _____ pointed.

   a. much   b. more

Check True or False

1. They both have bumpy skin.

   T ☐   F ☐

2. Crocodiles have rounded snouts.

   T ☐   F ☐

3. Crocodiles live in America, Asia, Africa, and Australia.

   T ☐   F ☐

Story Comprehension

1 What's the main idea?

　　a. Reptiles

　　b. Alligators

　　c. Alligators and crocodiles

2 They have _____ legs and long, _____ tails.

　　a. short - weak　　b. long - strong　　c. short - strong

3 Who have rounded snouts?

　　a. alligators　　　　b. crocodiles

4 Where does alligators live?

　　a. They live in Asia.

　　b. They live in Africa and Australia.

　　c. They live only in the United States and China.

5 What is true?

　　a. They are not reptiles.

　　b. They both have smooth skin.

　　c. Their snouts look rather different.

스토리 해석 및 정답

Unit 1

Key Expression　　9p
① cute kitten　　② large tree

 Story　　10p

애니는 그리는 것을 좋아해요.

나의 여동생 애니는 그리는 것을 좋아해요.
그녀는 강아지를 그려요.
정말 귀여운 강아지예요!
그녀는 나비를 그려요.
정말 아름다운 나비예요!
그녀는 꽃들을 그려요.
정말 화려한 꽃들이에요!
그녀는 자신을 그려요.
정말 사랑스런 소녀예요!
그녀는 훌륭한 화가예요.

 **Vocabulary**　　11p

Write the Words

① lovely　　② butterfly　　③ puppy
④ flower　　⑤ beautiful　　⑥ painter

Unscramble the Letters

① cute　　② draw

 After Reading　　12~13p

Look and Check

① b　　② a　　③ a

Number the Sentences
a. ②　　b. ③　　c. ①

Choose the Correct Words
① b　　② b　　③ b

Check True or False
① T　　② T　　③ F

Story Comprehension　　14p

① c　　② c　　③ b
④ c　　⑤ a

Unit 2

Key Expression　　15p
① ② various

Story　　16p

날씨

다양한 날씨가 있어요.
봄은 따뜻해요.
여름은 더워요.
가을은 시원해요.
겨울은 추워요.
날씨는 항상 변해요.
때로는 화창해요.
때로는 구름이 껴요.
때로는 바람이 불고 비가 와요.
때로는 눈이 와요.

Vocabulary   17p

Write the Words

① warm   ② cloudy   ③ rainy
④ autumn   ⑤ spring   ⑥ windy

Unscramble the Letters

① weather   ② cool

After Reading   18~19p

Look and Check

① a   ② a   ③ a

Number the Sentences

a. ①   b. ③   c. ②

Choose the Correct Words

① b   ② b   ③ a

Check True or False

① F   ② T   ③ T

Story Comprehension   20p

① b   ② a   ③ c
④ c   ⑤ c

Unit 3

Key Expression   21p

① are, late   ② is, late

Story   22p

에릭은 이상한 소년이에요.

에릭은 이상한 소년이에요.
그는 다른 소년들과 달라요.
그는 항상 학교에 지각해요.
그는 종종 수업 시간에 듣지를 않아요.
그리고 그는 종종 공상에 잠겨요.
그의 선생님은 말씀하세요.
"에릭은 우리 학교에서 가장 나쁜 소년이다."
그러나 그는 가장 나쁜 소년이 아니에요.
그는 모든 것에 호기심이 많아요.
그리고 그는 상상력이 매우 풍부한 소년
이에요.
그는 결코 이상한 소년이 아니에요.

Vocabulary   23p

Write the Words

① late   ② weird   ③ school
④ listen   ⑤ curious   ⑥ imaginative

Unscramble the Letters

① class   ② daydream

After Reading   24~25p

Look and Check

① b   ② b   ③ b

Number the Sentences

a. ②   b. ①   c. ③

Choose the Correct Words
① a   ② b   ③ a

Check True or False
① T   ② F   ③ F

Story Comprehension   26p
① c   ② c   ③ c
④ a   ⑤ b

Unit 4

Key Expression   27p
① arrive at   ② arrived at

Story   28p

늑대와 수달

늑대는 큰 숲을 지나가면서 여행을 했어요.
늑대는 목이 너무 말랐고 배가 고팠어요.
늑대는 수달을 만났어요.
"물이 어디 있니?" 늑대가 말했어요.
"날 따라와." 수달이 말했어요.
늑대는 수달을 따라갔어요.
그들은 개울에 도착했어요.
늑대는 물을 마셨어요.
수달은 늑대에게 먹을 것도 주었어요.
늑대는 수달과 친구가 되었어요.

Vocabulary   29p

Write the Words
① forest   ② follow   ③ travel
④ wolf   ⑤ stream   ⑥ otter

Unscramble the Letters
① through   ② drink

After Reading   30~31p

Look and Check
① b   ② a   ③ a

Number the Sentences
a. ①   b. ②   c. ③

Choose the Correct Words
① b   ② a   ③ b

Check True or False
① T   ② F   ③ T

Story Comprehension   32p
① a   ② b   ③ c
④ c   ⑤ c

Unit 5

Key Expression   33p
① older   ② shorter

Story 34p

주디는 어른이 되고 싶어 해요.

주디는 어린 소녀예요.
그녀는 큰언니와 큰오빠가 있어요.
그녀의 언니, 제인은 주디보다 키가 커요.
그리고 그녀의 오빠, 제이크는 키가 훨씬
더 커요.
제이크는 멋진 스케이트보드가 있어요.
제인은 큰 자전거가 있어요.
주디는 작은 세발자전거가 있어요.
주디는 어른이 되고 싶어 해요.
그녀는 큰 자전거를 타고 싶어 해요.
그녀는 스케이트보드를 타고 싶어 해요.

Vocabulary 35p

Write the Words
① big   ② grow
③ bike   ④ much taller
⑤ skateboard   ⑥ taller

Unscramble the Letters
① little   ② tricycle

After Reading 36~37p

Look and Check
① b   ② b   ③ a

Number the Sentences
a. ③   b. ②   c. ①

Choose the Correct Words
① b   ② b   ③ a

Check True or False
① T   ② F   ③ T

Story Comprehension 38p

① b   ② c   ③ a
④ b   ⑤ b

Unit 6

Key Expression 39p
① deer   ② sheep

 **Story** 40p

할아버지의 마당

우리 할아버지와 할머니는 시골에 살아요.
그분들의 집에는 큰 마당이 있어요.
마당에는 놀이터가 있어요.
작은 연못도 있어요.
우리 할아버지께서 우리에게 그것들을 만
들어 주셨어요.
놀이터에는 트램펄린, 시소 그리고 그네
가 있어요. 연못에는 고기가 있어요.
우리는 놀이터에서 노는 것을 좋아해요.
그리고 연못에서 고기를 보는 것을 좋아
해요.
우리는 거기에 있는 게 너무 행복해요.

Vocabulary 41p

Write the Words

❶ yard   ❷ trampoline   ❸ swings

❹ pond   ❺ playground   ❻ seesaw

Unscramble the Letters

❶ country   ❷ fish

After Reading 42~43p

Look and Check

❶ b   ❷ a   ❸ a

Number the Sentences

a. ❶   b. ❸   c. ❷

Choose the Correct Words

❶ a   ❷ a   ❸ b

Check True or False

❶ T   ❷ T   ❸ F

Story Comprehension 44p

❶ b   ❷ c   ❸ a

❹ a   ❺ c

Unit 7

Key Expression 45p

❶ want to be   ❷ wants to be

Story 46p

케빈은 꿈이 많아요.

케빈은 종종 꿈이 바뀌어요.

때때로 그는 매우 유명해지길 원해요.

그래서 영화 배우가 되려고 해요.

때때로 그는 우주에 대해서 알고 싶어 해요.

그래서 우주비행사가 되려고 해요.

때때로 그는 부자가 되길 원해요.

그래서 사업가가 되려고 해요.

그리고 때때로 그는 피아노를 연주하길 원해요.

그래서 피아니스트가 되려고 해요.

Vocabulary 47p

Write the Words

❶ astronaut   ❷ movie star

❸ universe   ❹ businessman

❺ pianist   ❻ rich

Unscramble the Letters

❶ piano   ❷ famous

After Reading 48~49p

Look and Check

❶ b   ❷ b   ❸ b

Number the Sentences

a. ❶   b. ❷   c. ❸

Choose the Correct Words
① b ② b ③ b

Check True or False
① F ② T ③ F

 Story Comprehension 50p

① c ② b ③ a
④ c ⑤ b

Unit 8

Key Expression 51p
① ② join

Story 52p

그는 코를 골기 시작했어요.

잭과 나는 여름캠프에 참가했어요.
우리는 산꼭대기까지 도보여행을 했어요.
그리고나서 우리 힘으로 저녁요리를 했어요.
그래서 우리는 매우 피곤했어요.
잭과 나는 텐트로 갔어요.
곧 잭은 잠들었지만, 난 그렇지 않았어요.
왜냐하면 그가 코를 골기 시작해서였어요.
나는 더 이상 참을 수가 없었어요.
그래서 일어나 텐트에서 밖으로 나왔어요.
나는 밤새도록 깨어 있었어요.

 Vocabulary 53p

Write the Words
① camp ② tent ③ top
④ hike ⑤ snore ⑥ awake

Unscramble the Letters
① dinner ② join

After Reading 54~55p

Look and Check
① b ② a ③ b

Number the Sentences
a. ① b. ③ c. ②

Choose the Correct Words
① b ② a ③ b

Check True or False
① F ② T ③ T

Story Comprehension 56p

① c ② a ③ c
④ b ⑤ a

Unit 9

Key Expression 57p
① ② can

Story 58p

샘은 겁내지 않았어요.

샘은 겁이 많은 소년이에요.
그리고 그의 친구 제이크는 용감한 소년
이에요.
어느 날, 그들은 근처에 있는 개울가에 갔
어요.
개울가에는 징검다리가 있어요.
제이크는 돌 위를 뛰어올라 갔어요.
제이크는 말했어요.
"이리 와, 샘. 넌 할 수 있어."
샘은 숨을 깊게 내쉬었어요.
"난 할 수 있어." 샘이 말했어요.
그리고는 그도 돌 위를 뛰어올라 갔어요.
마침내, 그는 해냈어요.
샘은 행복해 했어요.
샘은 겁내지 않았어요.

 **Vocabulary** 59p

Write the Words

① step   ② timid   ③ nearby
④ brave   ⑤ stone

Unscramble the Letters

① breath   ② scared

 After Reading 60~61p

Look and Check

① a   ② a   ③ a

Number the Sentences

a. ②   b. ③   c. ①

Choose the Correct Words

① a   ② b   ③ b

Check True or False

① F   ② T   ③ F

 **Story Comprehension** 62p

① c   ② a   ③ c   ④ b   ⑤ a

Unit 10

Key Expression 63p

① gave, gift   ② gave, computer

 Story 64p

나는 너를 사랑해, 보라색 기린아!

오늘은 신디의 생일이었어요.
그녀는 아빠가 신디에게 보라색 기린을
주었어요.
그녀는 이 선물을 보고 매우 기뻐했어요.
신디는 보라색 기린을 사랑했어요.
신디는 말했어요.
"나는 너를 사랑해, 보라색 기린아!"
그녀는 보라색 기린에게 키스했어요.
그녀는 기린과 함께 과자를 먹었어요.
그녀는 기린과 함께 책을 읽었어요.
그녀는 항상 기린과 함께 놀았어요.
그리고 신디는 기린과 함께 잠자리에 들
었어요.

Vocabulary 65p

Write the Words
1 birthday 2 cookie 3 gift
4 giraffe 5 purple

Unscramble the Letters
1 glad 2 kiss

 After Reading 66~67p

Look and Check
1 b 2 b 3 b

Number the Sentences
a. 2 b. 3 c. 1

Choose the Correct Words
1 b 2 a 3 b

Check True or False
1 F 2 F 3 T

Story Comprehension 68p

1 b 2 a 3 b
4 a 5 c

Unit 11

Key Expression 69p
1 loves to play 2 love to study

 Story 70p

애니는 텔레비전을 보는 것을 좋아해요.

애니는 텔레비전을 보는 것을 좋아해요.
특히, 그녀는 음악쇼 프로그램을 좋아해요.
애니는 TV에 나오는 팝 가수처럼 노래 부르는 것을 좋아해요.
그리고 그녀는 백 댄서처럼 춤을 춰요.
그녀는 춤을 추면서 노래를 꽤 잘 불러요.
애니는 종종 TV에서 드라마를 봐요.
애니는 배우처럼 연기해요.
그녀는 연기도 꽤 잘 해요.
애니의 친구들은 그녀의 춤과 노래를 좋아해요.
그녀는 훌륭한 연예인이 될 거예요.

Vocabulary 71p

Write the Words
1 act 2 actor 3 show
4 television 5 dancer 6 entertainer

Unscramble the Letters
1 singer 2 drama

After Reading 72~73p

Look and Check
1 a 2 b 3 a

Number the Sentences
a. 1 b. 2 c. 3

Choose the Correct Words
① a   ② b   ③ b

Check True or False
① T   ② F   ③ F

 Story Comprehension   74p

① b   ② b   ③ c
④ b   ⑤ c

Unit 12

Key Expression   75p
① getting old   ② getting cold

Story   76p

그들은 괜찮았어요.

소년과 소녀는 소풍을 갔어요.
그들은 좋은 시간을 보냈어요.
그러나 날이 점점 어두워져갔어요.
그들은 집으로 돌아가야만 했어요.
그들은 지름길로 가기로 결심했어요.
그들은 기찻길을 따라 걸어갔어요.
매우 위험했어요.
왜냐하면 가끔 기차가 오기 때문이에요.
조금 후에, 기차가 왔어요.
그들은 기찻길을 벗어났어요.
기차가 지나갔고, 그들은 괜찮았어요.

 Vocabulary   77p

Write the Words
① shortcut   ② train   ③ dark
④ go back   ⑤ down   ⑥ dangerous

Unscramble the Letters
① track   ② pass

After Reading   78~79p

Look and Check
① a   ② b   ③ a

Number the Sentences
a. ①   b. ②   c. ③

Choose the Correct Words
① b   ② a   ③ a

Check True or False
① T   ② F   ③ F

Story Comprehension   80p

① c   ② a   ③ b
④ b   ⑤ a

Unit 13

Key Expression   81p
① ② tried to

Story   82p

원숭이 한 마리로는 충분하지 않아요.

원숭이 두 마리가 나무 위에서 놀았어요.
그들은 표범을 조심해야 되었어요.
그러나 원숭이들은 너무 졸려서 표범에
대해 잊어버렸어요.
그들 둘 다 낮잠을 잤어요.
배고픈 표범은 점심을 찾고 있어요.
마침 그는 원숭이 두 마리를 발견했어요.
그는 매우 배가 고팠어요.
그는 생각했어요.
"원숭이 한 마리로는 충분하지 않아"
그는 원숭이 두 마리를 원했어요.
그는 둘 다 잡으려고 했어요.
그러나 원숭이 두 마리는 도망갔어요.

Vocabulary   83p

Write the Words

① catch   ② look for   ③ nap
④ leopard   ⑤ lunch   ⑥ run away

Unscramble the Letters

① forget   ② monkey

After Reading   84~85p

Look and Check

① b   ② b   ③ b

Number the Sentences

a. ③   b. ②   c. ①

Choose the Correct Words

① b   ② b   ③ a

Check True or False

① T   ② F   ③ T

Story Comprehension   86p

① b   ② b   ③ a
④ c   ⑤ c

Unit 14

Key Expression   87p

① ② put on

Story   88p

어느 겨울 아침

어느 겨울 아침, 샐리는 일어났어요.
그녀는 창밖을 보았어요.
눈이 오고 있었어요.
눈은 모든 것을 덮었어요.
그녀는 아침을 빨리 먹었어요.
아침을 먹은 후에, 그녀는 눈옷을 입었어
요. 그리고 그녀는 밖으로 뛰어 나갔어요.
그녀는 친구들을 만났어요.
그녀는 친구들과 함께 눈사람을 만들었
어요.
그리고 눈싸움을 했어요.
몹시 추웠지만, 매우 재미있었어요.

Number the Sentences

a. ③   b. ①   c. ②

Choose the Correct Words

① b   ② b   ③ b

Check True or False

① F   ② T   ③ T

Story Comprehension   98p

① b   ② c   ③ a
④ c   ⑤ c

Unit 16

Key Expression   99p

①② grow

Story   100p

식물들

동물들은 입으로 물을 마시고 음식을 먹어요.
식물들은 어떻게 물을 마시고 음식을 먹
을까요?
식물들은 뿌리들, 줄기들, 잎들이 있어요.
뿌리들은 땅 속에서 자라요.
잎들과 줄기들은 땅 위에서 자라요.
뿌리들은 물과 음식을 흡수해요
줄기들은 뿌리에서 위쪽으로 자라요.
뿌리들과 줄기들은 잎과 같이 연결되어
있어요.

잎들은 음식을 만들기 위한 해의 에너지
로 사용해요.
그것들은 음식을 만들기 위해 함께 일해요.

Vocabulary   101p

Write the Words

① ground   ② stem   ③ leaf
④ root   ⑤ plant   ⑥ absorb

Unscramble the Letters

① under   ② mouth

After Reading   102~103p

Look and Check

① b   ② b   ③ b

Number the Sentences

a. ②   b. ③   c. ①

Choose the Correct Words

① a   ② a   ③ b

Check True or False

① F   ② T   ③ T

Story Comprehension   104p

① b   ② b   ③ b
④ a   ⑤ b

Unit 17

Key Expression 105p
① be an astronaut ② be a teacher

Story 106p

줄리아의 가족은 동물원에 갔어요.

줄리아와 그녀의 가족은 동물원에 갔어요.
그들은 코끼리를 봤어요.
코는 매우 강하고 유용했어요.
코로 모든 걸 했어요.
줄리아의 엄마는 사슴 보는 걸 좋아했어요.
사슴뿔은 우아했어요.
줄리아의 엄마는 사슴 사진을 찍었어요.
줄리아와 그녀의 오빠는 돌고래를 보는
걸 좋아했어요.
돌고래 쇼는 환상적이었어요.
조련사들과 돌고래들은 훌륭했어요.
줄리아는 동물 조련사가 되고 싶었어요.

Vocabulary 107p

Write the Words

① elephant   ② trainer
③ antler   ④ deer
⑤ zoo   ⑥ dolphin

Unscramble the Letters

① photo   ② trunk

After Reading 108~109p

Look and Check
① a   ② b   ③ b

Number the Sentences
a. ③   b. ①   c. ②

Choose the Correct Words
① b   ② b   ③ b

Check True or False
① T   ② F   ③ T

Story Comprehension 110p
① a   ② a   ③ c
④ b   ⑤ c

Unit 18

Key Expression 111p
① when, begins ② what, has

Story 112p

자유의 여신상을 아나요?

자유의 여신상을 아나요?
조각상이 어디에 있는지 아나요?
조각상을 누가 만들었는지 아나요?
조각상이 언제 만들어졌는지 아나요?
조각상이 무엇을 나타내는지 아나요?

조각상은 뉴욕의 자유섬에 있어요.
프랑스 조각가가 그것을 만들었어요.
1884에 만들었어요.
그리고 그것은 같은 년도에 미국으로 기증했어요.
오늘날 자유의 여신상은 자유를 나타내요.

Vocabulary 113p

Write the Words

① when ② where ③ sculptor
④ statue ⑤ who ⑥ what

Unscramble the Letters

① French ② island

After Reading 114~115p

Look and Check

① b ② a ③ a

Number the Sentences

a. ① b. ② c. ③

Choose the Correct Words

① b ② a ③ b

Check True or False

① T ② F ③ T

Story Comprehension 116p

① c ② c ③ a
④ a ⑤ a

Unit 19

Key Expression 117p

① prettier than ② better than

Story 118p

우리는 운동회를 했어요.

오늘은 운동회 날이었어요.
피터는 축구를 잘하지 못해요.
그는 배구도 역시 잘하지 못해요.
그러나 야구는 다른 사람들보다 잘 할 수 있어요.
그래서 그는 선수들 중 한 명으로 선발되었어요.
피터와 조원들은 최선을 다했어요.
그리고 그의 팀이 야구 경기에서 이겼어요.
피터는 매우 행복했어요.
그의 반은 다른 경기에서는 이기지 못했어요.
그러나 피터는 야구 경기에서 승리해 행복했어요.

Vocabulary 119p

Write the Words

① volleyball ② player
③ soccer ④ choose
⑤ baseball ⑥ win

Unscramble the Letters

① field ② team

After Reading 120~121p

Look and Check
① b   ② a   ③ a

Number the Sentences
a. ③   b. ②   c. ①

Choose the Correct Words
① b   ② a   ③ b

Check True or False
① T   ② F   ③ F

Story Comprehension 122p

① a   ② c   ③ b
④ b   ⑤ b

Unit 20

Key Expression 123p
① looks, tired   ② looks, beautiful

 Story 124p

앨리게이터들과 크로커다일들

앨리게이커들과 크로커다일들을 너는 아니?
그들은 파충류들이야.
그들은 둘 다 울퉁불퉁한 피부가 있어.
짧은 다리와 길고 강한 꼬리가 있어.
그들은 둘 다 수영을 잘 해.

그러나 코가 약간 달라.
앨리게이터는 둥근 코를 가지고 있어.
크로커다일의 코는 더 뾰족해.
앨리게이터는 미국이나 중국에서만 살아.
크로커다일은 미국, 아시아, 아프리카, 오
스트레일리아에서 살아.

 Vocabulary 125p

Write the Words
① rounded   ② reptile   ③ snout
④ pointed   ⑤ bumpy   ⑥ strong

Unscramble the Letters
① alligator   ② crocodile

After Reading 126~127p

Look and Check
① a   ② a   ③ b

Number the Sentences
a. ③   b. ②   c. ①

Choose the Correct Words
① a   ② b   ③ b

Check True or False
① T   ② F   ③ T

Story Comprehension 128p

① c   ② c   ③ a
④ c   ⑤ c